思展
方程式

MW01699290

啓蒙級 1

萌芽級 2 躍進級 3 信心級 4 實力級 5

基礎漢字500

Basic Chinese 500

思展兒童文化社有限公司
SAGE FOUNDATION INTELLECT LIMITED
www.sagebooks.hk

目 錄
Contents

www.sagebooks.hk

免費下載
家長導讀及使用手冊(pdf)
全文普通話朗讀(mp3)

序

知識就是力量。知識就是財富。

求知欲要從娃娃開始培養。

《思展方程式》：

是最適合娃娃心智的識字法；

是兒童教育的實踐結晶；

是漢字邏輯的精華。

《基礎漢字500》：是獻給娃娃的。

本冊介紹給娃娃識字啟蒙的 20 個中文字。

娃娃看圖、明意、識字，並培養起他們閱讀的興致和樂趣。

祝願每個孩子的心智與情商與日俱長。

Foreword

Knowledge is power. Knowledge is wealth.

The desire to learn should be cultivated in early childhood.

"Sage Formula":

- An efficient method to learn to read Chinese
- Best adapted to a young child's learning pattern
- The result of years of practice in child education
- The essence of the Chinese writing system

We dedicate the "Sage Formula" series to all young children.

In this book, the child will learn to read 20 Chinese characters as a beginning reader. The pictures supply context and meaning to the words. Through these pictures and words, the child develops the love and joy of reading.

We wish every child a healthy development – both intellectually and emotionally.

再版序

《基礎漢字500》於2007年出版以來，得到了廣大家長和教師們的認同和支持。我們欣喜地聽到大家反映孩子們都喜愛自動拿《基礎漢字500》來看、喜愛高聲朗讀課文；課文裡的漢字學過就會記得。孩子們的進步就是我們最大的滿足。

《啟蒙級》初版以來，家長和教師們給了我們很多意見，指出了一些錯漏的地方。據此，我們在新版中作出了若干修改，希望能進一步迎合孩子們學習的需要。

我們衷心期望能繼續聽到大家的寶貴意見，和孩子們讀書的朗朗之聲。

Foreword to the new edition

Since Basic Chinese 500 was first published in 2007, we have received many positive comments and much support from parents and teachers. We are pleased to hear that children love to read from Basic Chinese 500, and that they enjoy reading the text out loud. We are also pleased to know that children are willing to repeatedly read the books, and that they can remember the words that they have learnt from the books. Such progress of the child is the best reward to all of us.

We have made several adjustments to this new edition according to some of the recommendations and requests from parents and teachers. We hope such adjustments will be better adapted to the child's learning.

Happy reading!

作者簡介

劉俐，職業兒童教育工作者。80年代於美國攻讀企業管理及電腦應用資訊科學，獲學士學位。其後又取得語言文字翻譯及傳譯碩士學位。繼而歷時十餘年專研語言學、兒童心理學、兒童教育學、及特殊兒童教育培訓。劉女仕先後於美國、日本、英國及法國接受兒童教育特殊培訓，持有「蒙台梭利兒童教育」國際文憑，並從實踐中創建出獨特的系列文化產品和相應的教學方法，能更有效地加快兒童心智的開發。劉女仕目前致力兒童文學創作，其作品有「遊戲啟蒙」、「遊戲啟閱」、「遊戲啟智」及一系列兒童故事等。

Author - Lucia L. Lau

Lucia is a child educator. She holds an international diploma in Montessori Early Childhood Education. She also holds a Master's degree in Translation and Interpretation. She has devoted more than 10 years in the studies of linguistics, child psychology, child education, as well as education for special needs children. Through observation, practice and analysis, she developed unique cultural products and corresponding teaching methods to foster children's intellectual development. Lucia likes to write for children. Her writings includes a collection of children's stories, "Games for Learning", "Games for Reading" and "Games for Exploring".

思展方程式簡介

「思展方程式」基礎漢字500是一套專為學前兒童而設計的漢字識字法。「思展方程式」透過對現代漢字應用的深入研究和分析，配合幼兒成長的生理和心理特點以及他們的學習模式，再經過實踐應用而產生，是一套嶄新的科學識字法。「思展方程式」的識字方法採選了500個兒童日常生活和兒童文學中最常出現的中文字，以字的常用頻率和兒童的理解能力作為基準，分成五個水平階段，讓孩子循序漸進地學習認讀和理解漢字。這五個階段分別為：啟蒙級、萌芽級、躍進級、信心級和實力級。課程的設計讓孩子在很短時間內就可以初步掌握兒童圖書中出現的大部份字，幫助他們早日達到獨立閱讀的能力。孩子從每課中都會學到一個新的字，然後這個字在接下來的每課中都會再重覆出現，讓孩子反覆練習，鞏固對每個生字的認識。

Sage Formula

The "Sage Formula" Basic Chinese 500 is a method specially developed and formulated for young children to learn Chinese. It is a scientific method which has been developed through in-depth research and analysis of the pragmatic use of modern Chinese. It takes into consideration a young child's physical and mental developments and his/her unique way of learning. It has selected 500 Chinese words which are most frequently used in children's literature and most relevant to a young child's day-to-day life. These words are grouped and arranged into 5 levels (Beginning, Budding, Building, Confident and Fluent) according to the frequency of usage and a young child's mental development. It is designed to help the child to learn most of the words appearing in children's story books within a short period of time. This encourages independent reading at an early age. The child learns a new word from each lesson. This word will then be repeated in subsequent lessons. This works like practices and the child builds a solid foundation and sound understanding of the use of the word.

第一課　四朵花

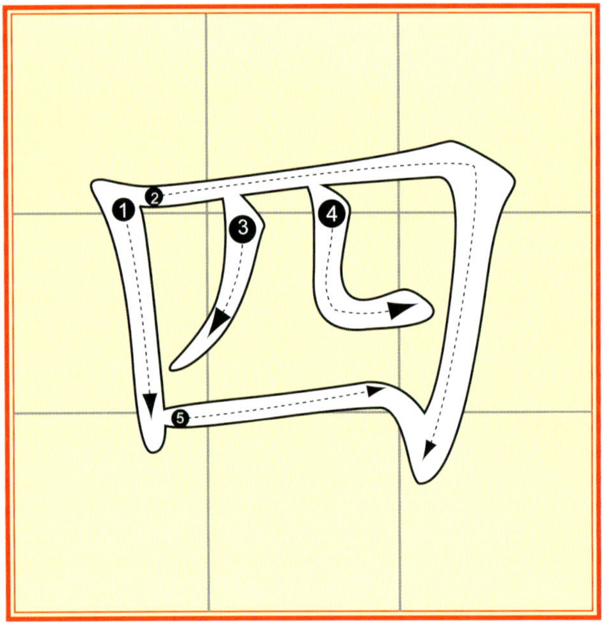

dì shang yǒu sì duǒ huā

地上有四朵花。

There are four flowers on the ground.

wǒ yǒu sì duǒ huā

我有四朵花。

I have four flowers.

nǐ yǒu wǔ duǒ xiǎo huā

你有五朵小花。

You have five flowers.

shān xia de huā hěn dà

山下的花很大。

The flowers at the bottom of the mountain are big.

wǒ men xià shān qù

我們下山去。

We go down the mountain.

完

The End

第二課　草

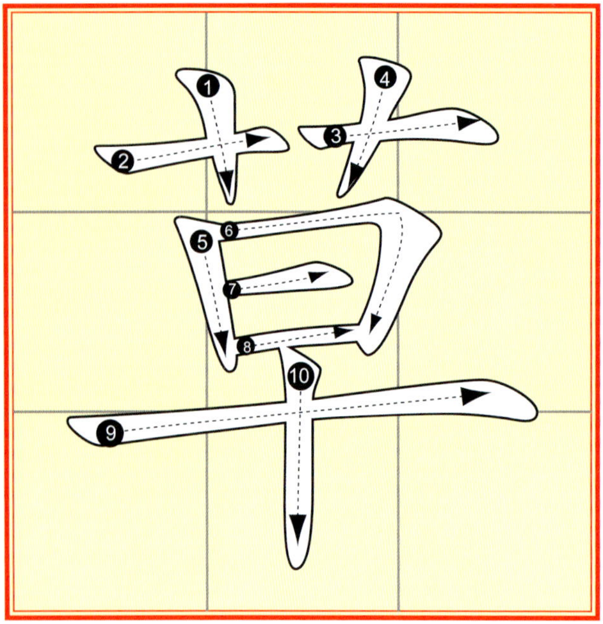

dì shang yǒu xiǎo cǎo

地上有小草。

There is grass on the ground.

dì shang yě yǒu xiǎo huā

地上也有小花。

There are also small flowers on the ground.

wǒ men zài cǎo dì shang

我們在草地上。

We are on the grass.

xiǎo mǎ yě zài cǎo dì shang

小馬也在草地上。

The foal is also on the grass.

xiǎo niǎo zài tiān shang

小鳥在天上。

The bird is in the sky.

完

The End

第三課　我到你家去

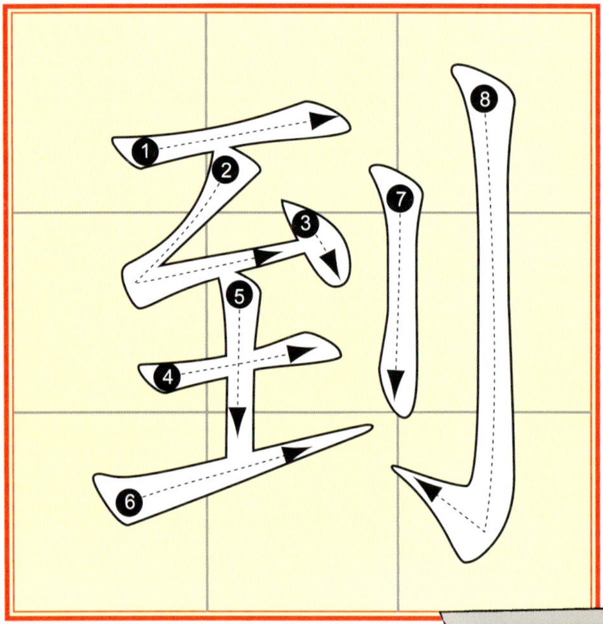

nǐ de jiā zài shān xia

你的家在山下。

Your home is at the bottom of the mountain.

wǒ dào nǐ jiā qù

我到你家去。

I go to your home.

shān xia yǒu cǎo dì

山下有草地。

There is grass at the bottom of the mountain.

cǎo dì shang yǒu huā duǒ

草地上有花朵。

There is a flower on the grass.

nǐ de jiā yǒu yì zhī xiǎo niǎo

你的家有一隻小鳥。

You have a little bird at home.

完

The End

第四課　我說

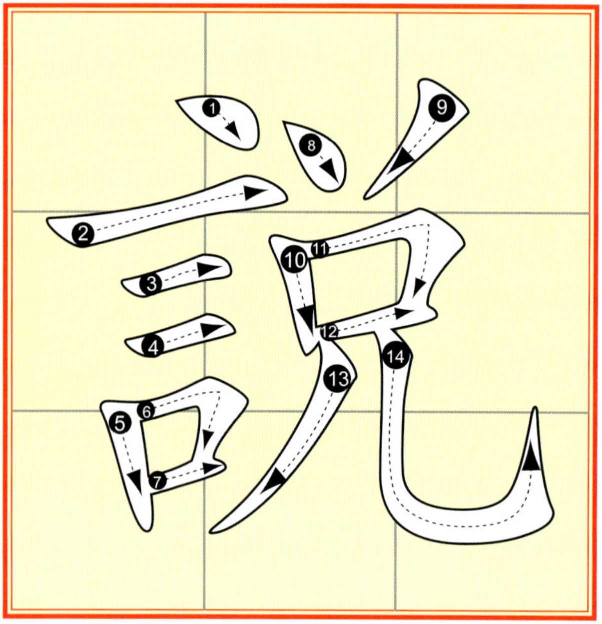

wǒ shuō wǒ dào shān xia qù

我說:「我到山下去。」

"I am going down the mountain," I said.

nǐ shuō dào wǒ jiā lái

你說：「到我家來。」

"Come to my home," you said.

mā ma shuō wǒ yě qù

媽媽説：「我也去。」

"I am also going," said Mother.

wǒ shuō zhè shì nǐ de

我說：「這是你的。」

"This is for you," I said.

wǒ men zài cǎo dì shang

我們在草地上。

We are on the grass.

完

The End

第五課　　好朋友

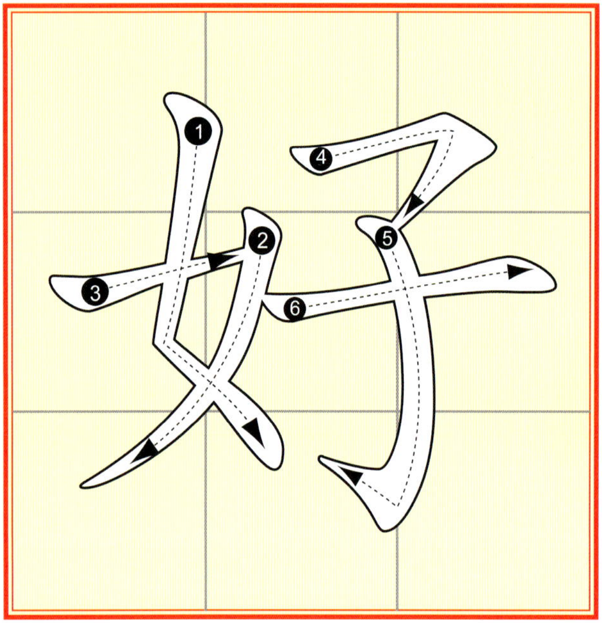

wǒ yǒu yí gè hǎo bà ba

我有一個好爸爸。

I have a good father.

wǒ yǒu yí gè hǎo mā ma

我有一個好媽媽。

I have a good mother.

nǐ shì wǒ de hǎo péng yǒu

你是我的好朋友。

You are my good friend.

tiān hǎo wǒ dào nǐ jiā qù

天好，我到你家去。

When the weather is fine, I go to your home.

tiān bù hǎo wǒ zài jiā

天不好，我在家。

When the weather is not good, I am at home.

完

The End

第六課　這是甚麼

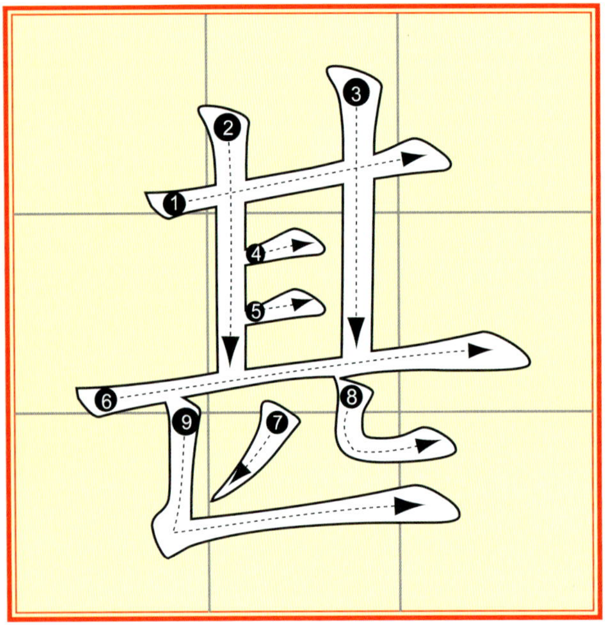

zhè shì shén me shì shǒu zhǐ

這是甚麼？是手指。

What is this? This is a finger.

zhè shì shén me shì niǎo

這是甚麼？是鳥。

What is this? This is a bird.

zhè shì shén me shì mǎ

這是甚麼？是馬。

What is this? This is a horse.

wǒ shuō nǐ shì hǎo péng yǒu

我說：「你是好朋友。」

"You are my good friend," I said.

nǐ shuō dào wǒ jiā lái

你說：「到我家來。」

"Come to my home," you said.

完

The End

第七課　地上有甚麼

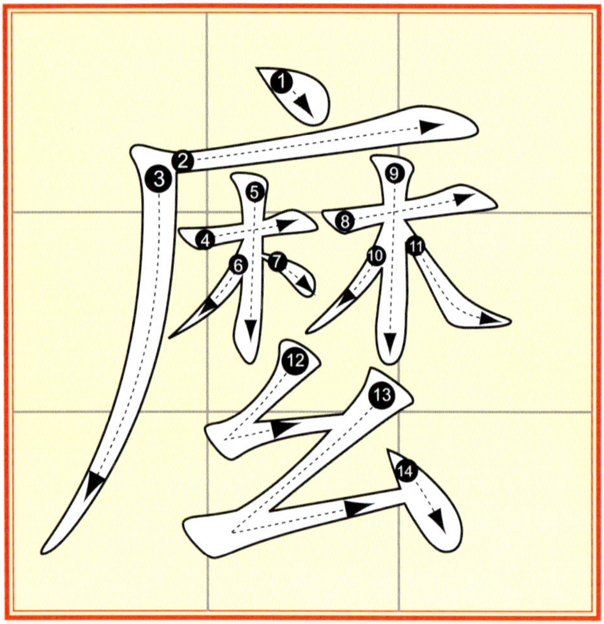

cǎo dì shang yǒu shén me

草地上有甚麼？

What is there on the grass?

yǒu huā duǒ， yǒu xiǎo cǎo

有花朵，有小草。

There are flowers, there is grass.

tiān shang yǒu shén me

天上有甚麼？

What is there in the sky?

tiān shang yǒu xiǎo niǎo

天上有小鳥。

There are birds in the sky.

wǒ men zài dì shang

我們在地上。

We are on the ground.

完

The End

第八課　小鳥在飛

xiǎo niǎo zài fēi

小鳥在飛。

The bird is flying.

liǎng zhī xiǎo niǎo fēi lái fēi qù

两隻小鳥飛來飛去。

Two birds are flying this way and that.

xiǎo mǎ fēi bú shàng tiān

小馬飛不上天。

The foal cannot fly in the sky.

wǒ men yě fēi bú shàng tiān

我們也飛不上天。

We cannot fly in the sky either.

nǐ shuō xiǎo niǎo zài tiān shang

你說：「小鳥在天上。」

"The bird is in the sky," you said.

完

The End

第九課　看

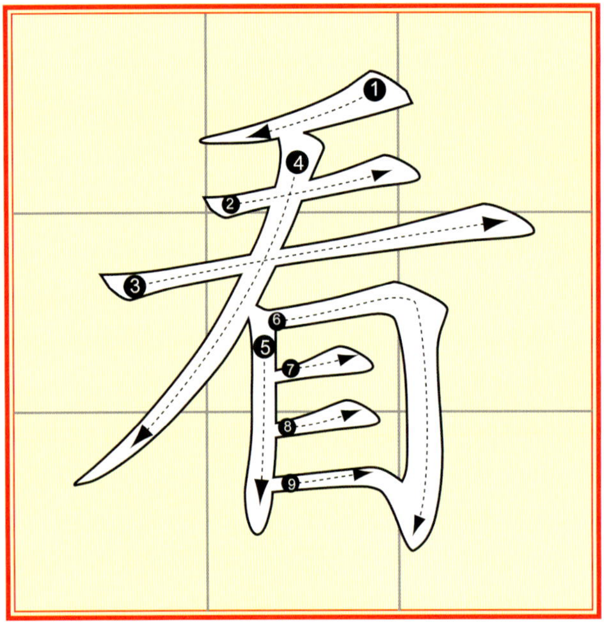

nǐ zài kàn shén me

你在看甚麼？

What are you looking at?

wǒ zài kàn cǎo dì shang de huā

我在看草地上的花。

I am looking at the flower on the grass.

zhè duǒ huā hěn hǎo kàn

這朵花很好看。

This flower is beautiful.

第十課　到這裏來

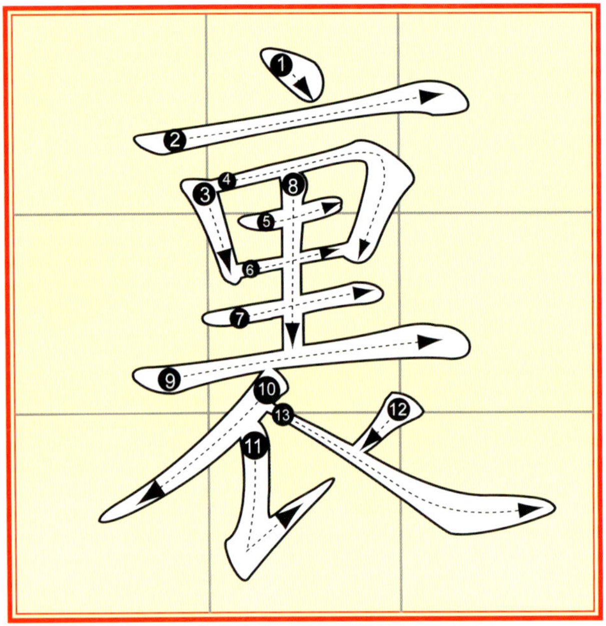

wǒ zài kàn huā

我在看花。

I am looking at the flower.

mā ma shuō dào zhè lǐ lái

媽媽說：「到這裏來。」

"Come here," said Mother.

wǒ shuō hǎo mǎ shàng lái

我説:「好,馬上來。」

"Yes, I am coming now," I said.

mā ma shǒu lǐ yǒu shén me

媽媽手裏有甚麼？

What has Mother got in her hands?

mā ma shǒu lǐ yǒu sì duǒ huā

媽媽手裏有四朵花。

Mother has got four flowers in her hands.

完

The End

第十一課　我們在一起

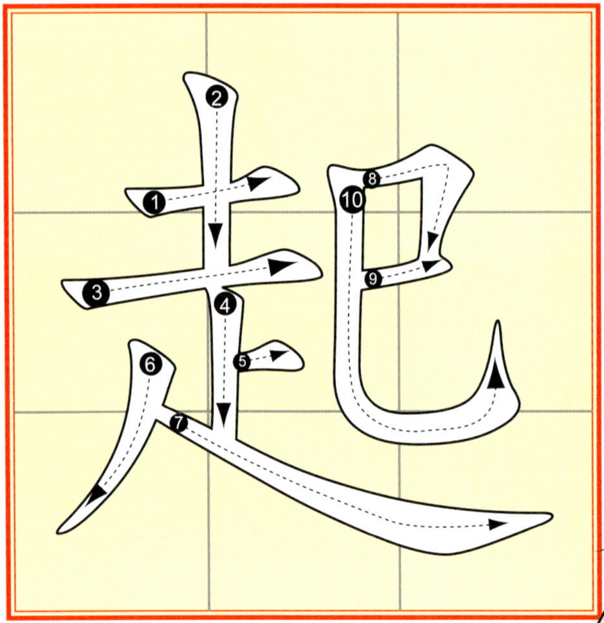

wǒ men liǎng gè rén zài yì qǐ

我們兩個人在一起。

The two of us are together.

bà ba mā ma zài yì qǐ

爸爸媽媽在一起。

Father and Mother are together.

dà jiā yì qǐ zài zhè lǐ

大家一起在這裏。

Everybody is here together.

wǒ men zài kàn shén me

我們在看甚麼？

What are we looking at?

wǒ men zài kàn xiǎo niǎo fēi

我們在看小鳥飛。

We are looking at the bird fly.

完

The End

第十二課　　我要飛

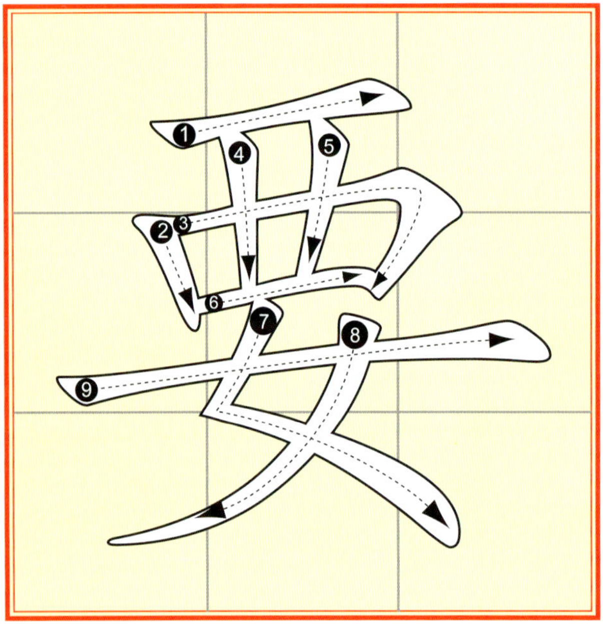

xiǎo niǎo shuō wǒ yào fēi

小鳥說：「我要飛。」

"I want to fly," said the little bird.

wǒ shuō wǒ yào qù kàn péng yǒu

我說：「我要去看朋友。」

"I want to go see my friend," I said.

bà ba shuō wǒ yě yào qù

爸爸說：「我也要去。」

"I want to go, too," said Father.

wǒ men yì qǐ dào nǐ de jiā

我們一起到你的家。

We go to your home together.

nǐ zài jiā lǐ

你在家裏。

You are at home.

完

The End

bà ba shì nán rén

爸爸是男人。

Father is a man.

zhè lǐ yǒu yí gè xiǎo nán hái
這裏有一個小男孩。

Here is a boy.

wǒ men dà jiā zài yì qǐ

我們大家在一起。

We are together.

wǒ men yào dào shān xia qu

我們要到山下去。

We want to go down the mountain.

完

The End

第十四課　小明

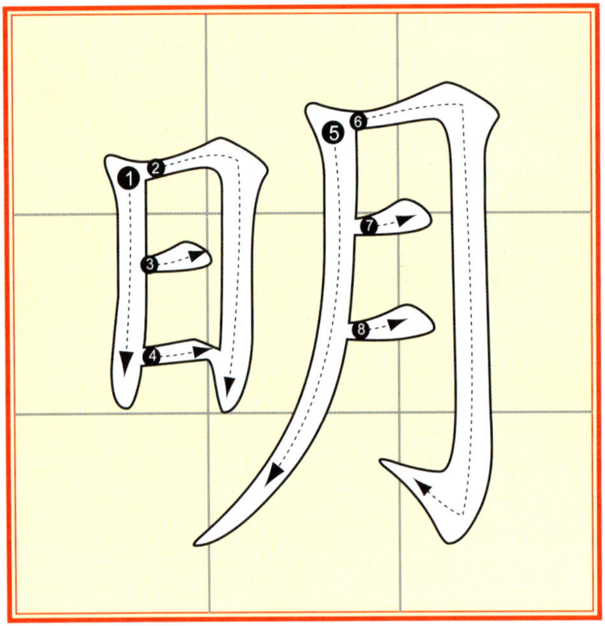

zhè shì xiǎo míng

這是小明。

This is Xiao Ming.

xiǎo míng shì wǒ de péng yǒu

小明是我的朋友。

Xiao Ming is my friend.

xiǎo míng shì gè xiǎo nán hái

小明是個小男孩。

Xiao Ming is a boy.

xiǎo míng jiā lǐ yǒu bà mā

小明家裏有爸媽。

Xiao Ming has a father and a mother.

wǒ men yì qǐ qù kàn xiǎo míng

我們一起去看小明。

We go to visit Xiao Ming together.

完

The End

第十五課　小兔

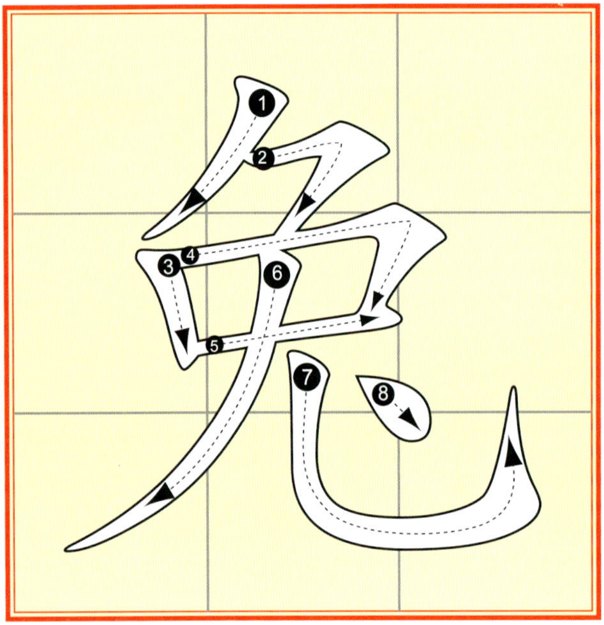

zhè shì shén me

這是甚麼？

What is this?

zhè shì yì zhī xiǎo tù

這是一隻小兔。

This is a little rabbit.

xiǎo tù zài cǎo dì shang

小兔在草地上。

The little rabbit is on the grass.

xiǎo míng yě zài yì qǐ

小明也在一起。

Xiao Ming is also here.

wǒ yào qù kàn xiǎo tù

我要去看小兔。

I want to go and see the little rabbit.

完

The End

第十六課　小白兔

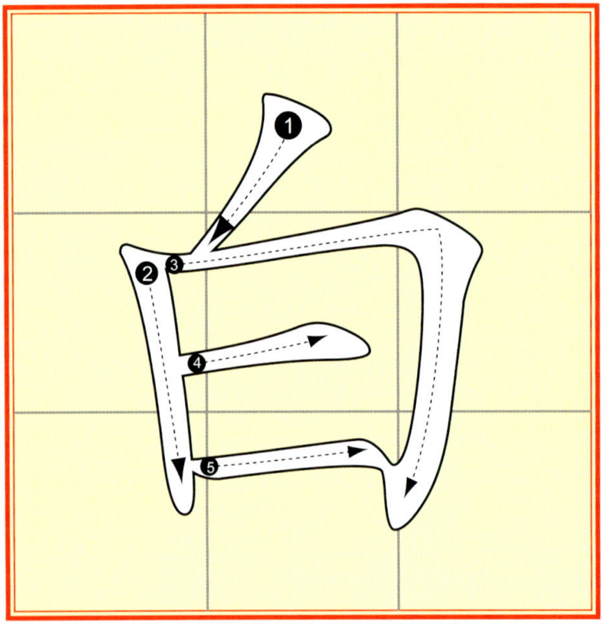

xiǎo míng shǒu lǐ yǒu xiǎo tù

小明手裏有小兔。

Xiao Ming has a little rabbit in his hands.

xiǎo tù hěn bái

小兔很白。

The little rabbit is very white.

xiǎo bái tù yào dào cǎo dì shang

小白兔要到草地上。

The little white rabbit wants to go on the grass.

xiǎo míng shì gè xiǎo nán hái

小明是個小男孩。

Xiao Ming is a boy.

wǒ men shì nǚ hái

我們是女孩。

We are girls.

完

The End

第十七課　看書

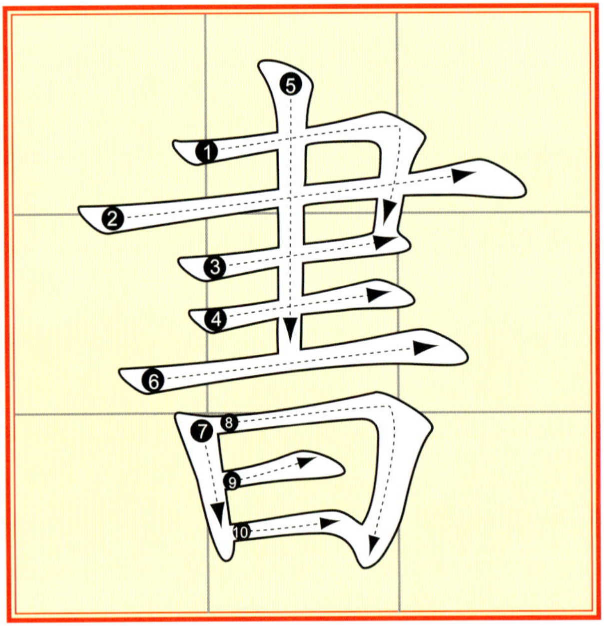

nǐ zài kàn shén me

你在看甚麼？

What are you looking at?

wǒ zài kàn shū

我在看書。

I am reading a book.

shū lǐ yǒu xiǎo bái tù

書裏有小白兔。

There is a little white rabbit in the book.

第十八課　一本書

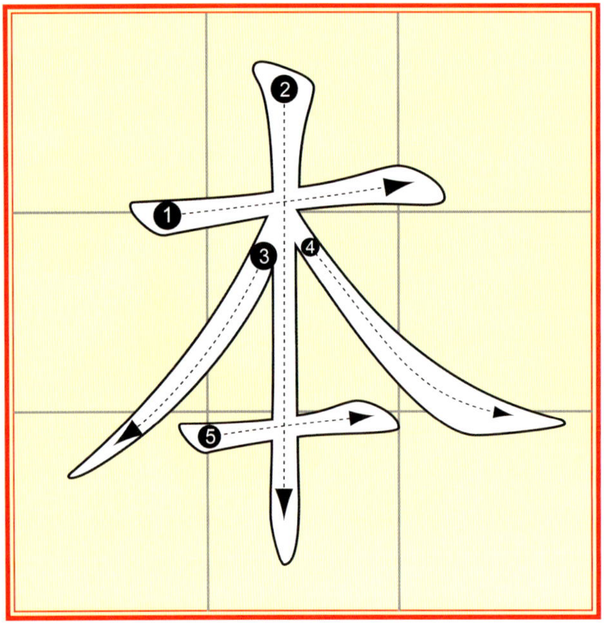

wǒ shǒu lǐ yǒu yì běn shū

我手裏有一本書。

I have a book in my hand.

nán hái yào kàn shū

男孩要看書。

Boys have to read books.

nǚ hái yě yào kàn shū

女孩也要看書。

Girls also have to read books.

yì rén yì běn shū

一人一本書。

One book for each person.

dà jiā yì qǐ kàn shū

大家一起看書。

We are reading together.

完

The End

第十九課　我會看書

wǒ huì kàn shū

我會看書。

I can read.

xiǎo bái tù bú huì kàn shū

小白兔不會看書。

The little white rabbit cannot read.

xiǎo niǎo huì fēi

小鳥會飛。

The little bird can fly.

xiǎo mǎ bú huì fēi

小馬不會飛。

The foal cannot fly.

liǎng gè rén kàn yì běn shū

兩個人看一本書。

Two people are reading one book.

完

The End

第二十課　吃甚麼

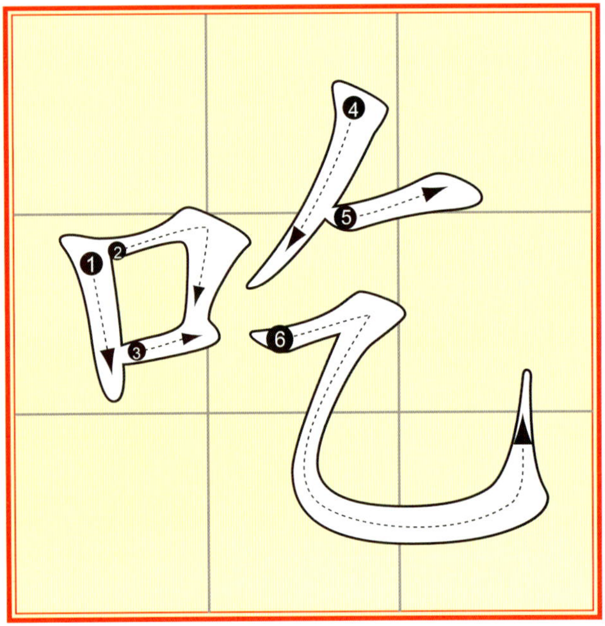

xiǎo bái tù zài chī shén me

小白兔在吃甚麼？

What is the little white rabbit eating?

xiǎo bái tù zài chī cǎo

小白兔在吃草。

The little white rabbit is eating grass.

xiǎo mǎ yě zài chī cǎo

小馬也在吃草。

The foal is also eating grass.

xiǎo míng bú yào chī cǎo

小明不要吃草。

Xiao Ming does not want to eat grass.

xiǎo nán hái zài chī shǒu zhǐ

小男孩在吃手指。

The little boy is sucking his finger.

完

The End

繪圖員簡介

文浩基 Mandom Man 職業小學教師。受其畫則師父親及日本漫畫影響，自幼熱衷於繪畫。學生時代開始曾任不同媒體兼職日語翻譯、繪畫插圖及設計工作。多年來參加各種創作、設計及繪畫比賽，並屢獲獎項。文老師放學後即活躍於畫紙及原稿紙上，參與出版的書刊近三十冊，是個不會停下來的創作人。

文珮珩 Samantha Man 兒童中心導師，興趣是繪畫和旅遊。小時候跟哥哥文浩基合作繪製多本漫畫及繪本供家人欣賞，兩兄妹便從此合作無間，更經常攜手參加不同類型的創作比賽，屢獲獎項。現活躍於兒童故事創作及角色設計的工作，為孩子們編出積極及美麗的夢，可說是一位編夢者。

豐富詞組及一字多義的100個字

躍進級 3

從具體事物進階到抽象概念的100個字

信心級 4

從自我世界走向社群生活的100個字

實力級 5

思展方程式

SAGE FORMULA

漫畫

成語

推動閱讀新紀元
iPhone/iPad應用程序
電子書
基礎漢字500
Basic Chinese
系列
基础汉字 1
基础汉字 2
基础汉字 3
基础汉字 4
基础汉字 5
十二生肖故事系列
龙公主
找秘密
DAISY'S
MYSTERY
Start
Setting
精彩出版 源源不絕~
Available on the
App Store

作者：劉俐
繪圖：文浩基
文珮珩

出版：思展兒童文化社有限公司
地址：香港荃灣海盛路11號
One Midtown 9樓15室
電話：+852-3529-1243
傳真：+852-2253-0528

國際書號： 978-988-17005-9-9

2007年7月　初版
2012年12月第四版

歡迎瀏覽本社網站：
www.sagebooks.hk

思展方程式
基礎漢字500
Basic Chinese

Author: Lucia L. Lau
Illustrator: Mandom Man
Samantha Man

ISBN: 978-988-17005-9-9

First edition July 2007
Fourth edition December 2012
Published in paperback in Hong Kong by Sage Foundation Intellect Limited

Please visit our website at:
www.sagebooks.hk